by
Peter Magadini

**Edited by
Wanda Sykes**

ISBN 0-634-03283-6

This publication was originally published in two volumes.
These volumes are now referred to as Part One and Part Two, which begins on page 31.

This book is dedicated to DON BOTHWELL

HAL•LEONARD®
CORPORATION

7777 W. BLUEMOUND RD. P.O. BOX 13819 MILWAUKEE, WI 53213

© 1993 by Peter Magadini
International Copyright Secured   All Rights Reserved

No part of this publication may be reproduced in any form or by any means without the prior written permission of the Publisher.

First printing of Volume One, January, 1967

Visit Hal Leonard Online at
www.halleonard.com

ABOUT THE AUTHOR

Peter Magadini is a professional percussionist, drummer, author and teacher.

Mr. Magadini holds a Bachelor of Music degree from the San Francisco Conservatory of Music and a Master of Music degree from the University of Toronto. In addition, he has studied with the North Indian master, Mahapurush Misra.

ABOUT THE BOOK

This book is a method designed to teach the creative musician and music student the art of playing polyrhythms. Literally, the word "polyrhythm" means "many rhythms." In common use the term means two or more rhythms played simultaneously, or *against* each other. Polyrhythms can also be thought of as two different meters (time signatures) played against (or more accurately, *with*) each other.*

*AUTHOR'S FOOTNOTE:

At the time volumes one and two of the original "Musician's Guide to Polyrhythms" were written, the word *"against"* was used to describe one rhythm simultaneously being played with another. During that period the word was used by musicians to describe very basic polyrhythmic functions (i.e. 3 against 2). However, to be more precise and accurate, the word *"against"* is better defined when thought of as meaning a rhythm that goes *"over," "under"* or *"with"* another rhythm which is played at the same time.

PART ONE

HOW TO USE THIS BOOK

METER (Beat):

To achieve the best results, the basic beat or meter must be kept absolutely consistent and unwavering. A metronome should be employed at the beginning of each section so the musician can concentrate fully on the counter rhythm. The relationship of the rhythms to each other will soon be heard and felt. The musician will then be able to use his own rhythm "feel" without the aid of the metronome.

COUNTING:

It is important to count each section as indicated. Many exercises will have two meters and, as a result, two counting patterns, occurring simultaneously. Counting as indicated is extremely important to the overall understanding of the exercise.

In order to understand a polyrhythm completely, the musician should try to count one rhythm aloud while playing the other. When the rhythmic relationships are fully understood and felt the process should be reversed, i.e., count the rhythm which was being played and play the other.

EXAMPLE:

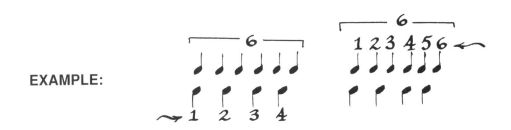

LISTENING:

The musician should memorize the sound of the basic counter rhythm against the basic meter as played on the same surface. He should also play on two different surfaces pitched an octave apart.

HOW TO PRACTICE

This book is adaptable for all instruments or none at all, whichever the musician prefers.

WITHOUT AN INSTRUMENT: To establish and understand polyrhythms without using a particular instrument, I suggest the musician clap his hands or use one hand on a flat surface to play the counter rhythm while a metronome maintains the basic pulse. When working without a metronome, use both hands - one for the counter rhythm and the other for the basic pulse. Two different sounding surfaces are suggested if this last method is used. The musician may also clap or sing one rhythm while his foot taps out the second rhythm.

PERCUSSION AND DRUMS: It is suggested that the student begin these studies on the drum pad using alternate sticking while the metronome maintains the basic meter. After the drummer feels secure with a particular section, he should then apply that section to the drum set using his feet, hi-hat and bass drum to keep the basic pulse. The drummer may also create his own combinations around the drums working out solo patterns from the book.

STRING AND WIND INSTRUMENTS: Here the musician should work out scale patterns and melodic ideas to fit the counter rhythms of the exercises in the book. The basic pulse can be maintained with a metronome or even by tapping the foot. The advantage of doing this is that the instrumentalist has a chance to apply and practice melodic ideas at the same time he is learning polyrhythms. Following is an example of how an exercise may be worked out:

EXAMPLE:

The top line of 12 notes is played as a sextuplet. The lower line of four notes represents the basic pulse in 4/4 meter. The example above simply applies a chromatic scale to the counter rhythm. The imaginative instrumentalist will soon discover the infinite melodic possibilities inherent in these counter rhythms.

PIANO: The pianist should follow the same general rules as those suggested for winds and strings. After the pianist feels sufficient confidence in his understanding of any rhythmic combination, he can use the right hand to play a melodic line corresponding rhythmically to the counter rhythm. The left hand will then play the basic pulse in either chordal or single line accompaniment. The reverse of this procedure also presents intriguing possibilities for improvisation.

The author's intent in writing this volume is to offer new and fresh ideas to any creative musician. If conscientious effort is applied, these rhythmic concepts cannot help but broaden horizons for the imaginative instrumentalist.

SECTION I
THREE AGAINST ONE

TRIPLETS:

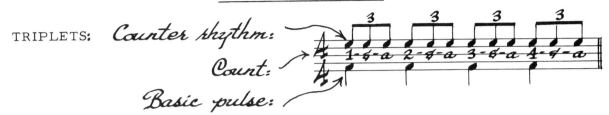

QUARTER NOTE TRIPLETS
THREE AGAINST TWO

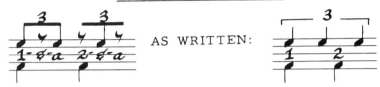

AS WRITTEN:

THREE AGAINST TWO = SIX AGAINST FOUR

AS WRITTEN: OR

EXERCISES

Vary tempos (slow, medium, fast)

Keep beat steady

EIGHTHS

EIGHTHS ADDED

EXERCISES

6

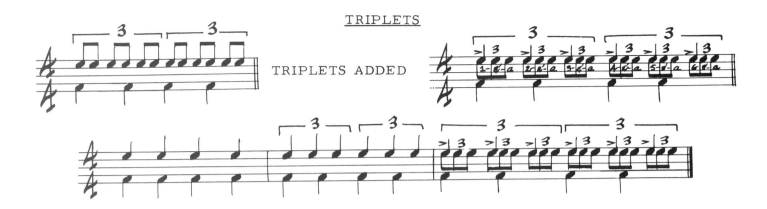

TRIPLETS ADDED

EXERCISES

SIXTEENTHS

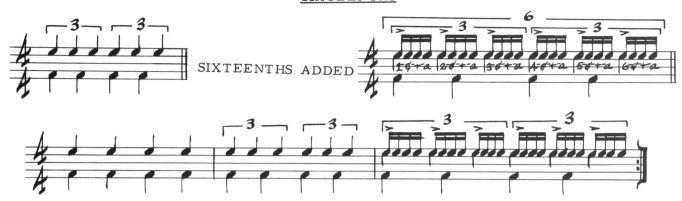

SIXTEENTHS ADDED

EXERCISES

8

COMBINATIONS*

*The bar lines have been purposely omitted in some Exercises and
Solos so the musician can feel and understand each of these exercises as a <u>continuous phrase</u>.

MIXED COMBINATIONS*

* You will note that the lower line of notes, the "Basic Pulse" has been omitted in some exercises and solos. The omission is intentional. The "Basic Pulse" or "Beat" must be played whether written or omitted.

SOLO

Flowing

SECTION II
THREE AGAINST FOUR

HALF NOTE TRIPLETS

AS WRITTEN

EXERCISES

QUARTERS

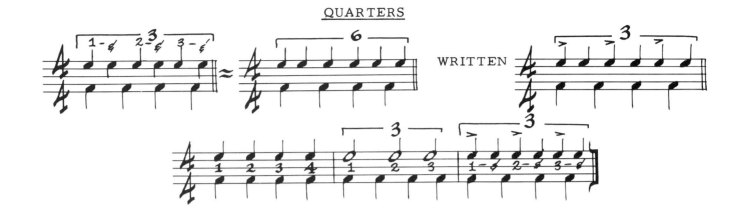

EXERCISES

IMPORTANT: Do not count 6!
Count only "1-and-2-and-3-and"
stressing accents.

EIGHTHS

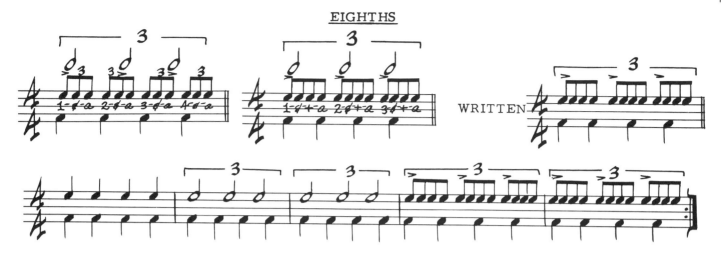

WRITTEN

EXERCISES

SIXTEENTHS

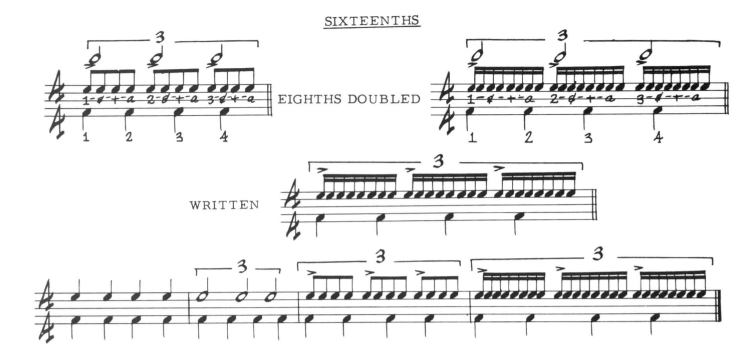

EIGHTHS DOUBLED

WRITTEN

EXERCISES

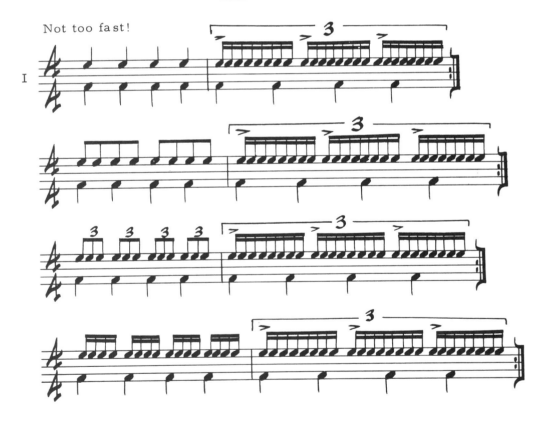

Not too fast!

I

EXERCISES (Cont.)

II

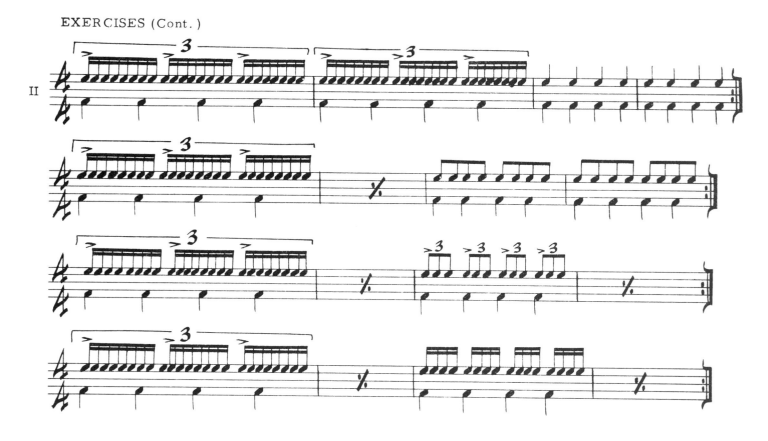

TRIPLETS

(Half note triplets divided in quarter note triplets.)

DIVIDE HALF NOTE INTO
QUARTER NOTE TRIPLETS:

NINE AGAINST FOUR

WRITTEN

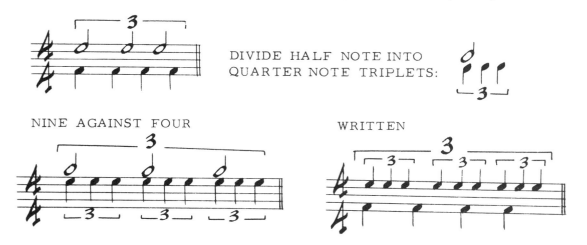

COMBINATIONS

MIXED COMBINATIONS

(Count carefully.)

SHORT COMBINATIONS

SOLO

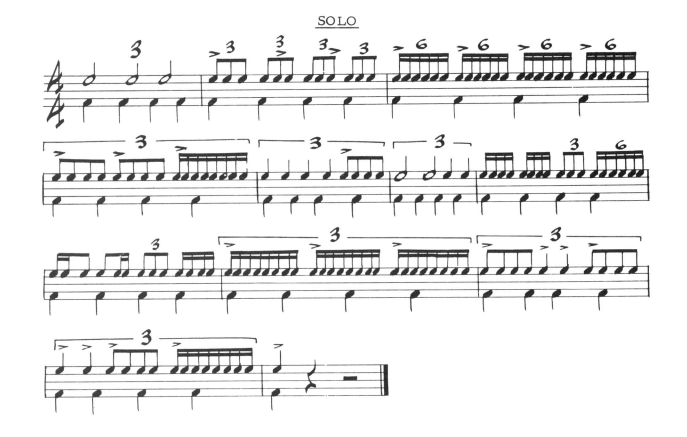

VARIED MIXED COMBINATIONS

SOLO

Do not count any measures in 6!
The basic Polyrhythm is:

SECTION III
FIVE AGAINST FOUR

AS WRITTEN

OR

It is important to try to learn to count 4 while playing 5. This is difficult.

EXERCISES

21

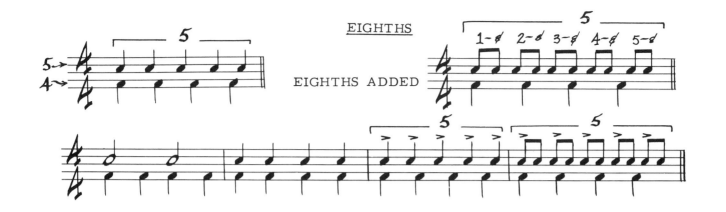

EIGHTHS

EIGHTHS ADDED

EXERCISES

22

TRIPLETS

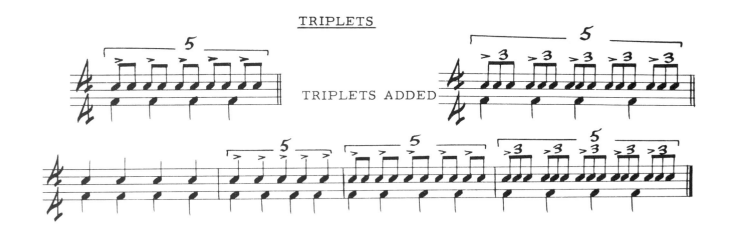

EXERCISES

SIXTEENTHS

SIXTEENTHS ADDED

EXERCISES

24

SHORT COMBINATIONS

MIXED COMBINATIONS

MIXED COMBINATIONS (Cont.)

SOLOS

NO BAR LINES

Practice slowly at first.

SECTION IV - SOLOS
Combines Sections I, II, and III.

Keep Solos flowing.

28

SOLOS (Cont.)

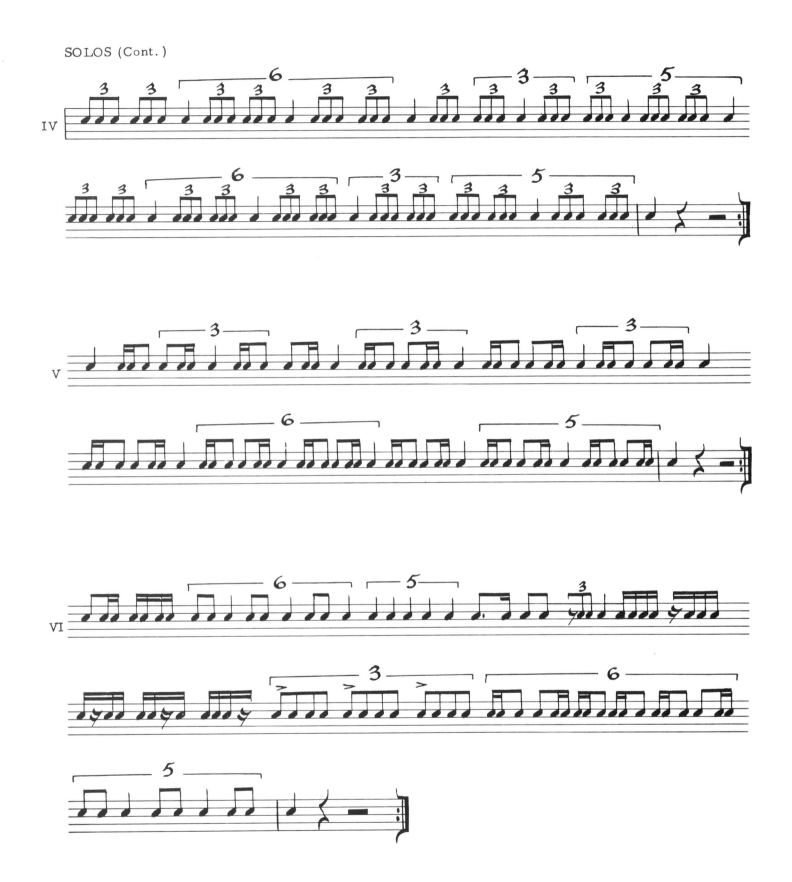

SOLOS (Cont.)

VII

Should be memorized.

VIII

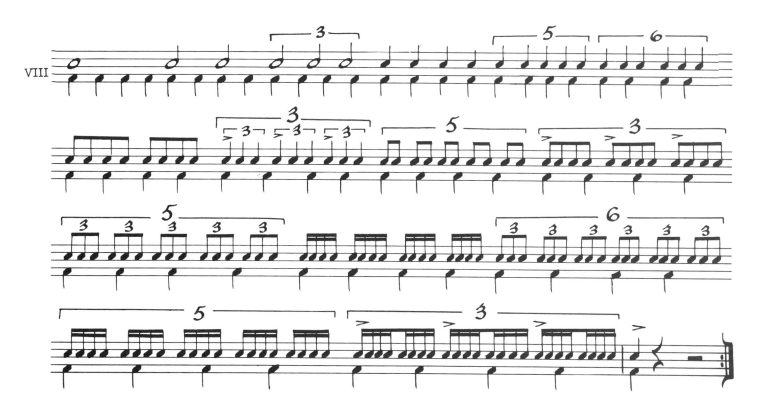

MORE ABOUT POLYRHYTHMS

Until recently, polyrhythmic concepts have been considered only incidental to western musical thought. The composers and performers who explored this facet of music to any degree usually gained their recognition through other aspects of their contributions to the art. True rhythmic freedom and polyrhythmic understanding, however, can finally be considered intrinsic elements in the music of our culture. Rhythmic studies are finally conceded to be important in the education of the serious music student.

In the 20th century, expanding awareness of cultures other than our own brought new musical and rhythmic conceptions to our attention. Studies of two widely different - yet curiously similar - musical cultures helped shape and advance the rhythmic sensitivity of the western musician. The first was the series of studies of the native music of Africa. These musical expeditions resulted in many magnificent recordings which were then made available to anyone interested. Westerners had previously thought of the music of Africa as only naive "drumming," nothing more than a primitive accompaniment to tribal ceremonies of a superstitious and unlettered people. A careful ear turned to the new recordings soon proved the fallacy of this attitude. The music, though almost exclusively percussion, revealed itself to be highly sophisticated, enormously complicated, exciting and beautiful.

Naturally there are great regional differences in the music of Africa, but some generalizations can nevertheless be made. Basically, the music is polyrhythmic. One finds every degree of complexity from a simple 6-against-4 Chant to extremely elaborate patterns of polymetric and polyrhythmic relationships between "voices." Frequently, more than two rhythms sound simultaneously creating contrapuntal layers of different meters and cross rhythms. Each layer flows at its own tempo and seems to be quite independent. The complex underlying structural organization is apparent when the layers of rhythm meet precisely and perfectly at predetermined points in the music.

Another equally important influence on western musical and rhythmic thought resulted from studies of the music of East India. The serious, contemporary music of East India derives from 4,000 years of musical tradition. The Master Musician in India dedicates his entire life to his art. This devotion results in a fantastic wealth of formal musical knowledge, a good part of which is the ability to improvise with extraordinary rhythmic and polyrhythmic dexterity and creativity. The music of India is delicate, beautiful, complex, and more demanding on the musician than any in the world.

Both these highly sophisticated forms of musical expression have influenced "Polyrhythms." The intention of this book, however, is to suggest rather than imitate the music of other cultures. The intention is also to present a practical method to extend the musical knowledge and sensitiveness of the contemporary musician by developing polyrhythmic techniques.

PART TWO

*AUTHOR'S FOOTNOTE:

Volume two, in its original form was dedicated to the memory of John Coltrane and Eric Dolphy. I would like to add the name Bob Yeager, the original publisher of these volumes.

SECTION 5

SEVEN AGAINST FOUR

AS WRITTEN:

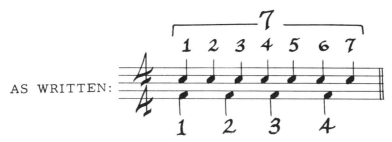

IT IS IMPORTANT TO LEARN TO COUNT 4 WHILE PLAYING 7.

EXERCISES

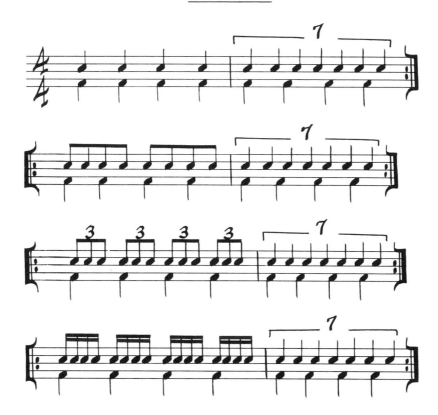

EXERCISES (Cont.)

EIGHTHS

EIGHTHS ADDED

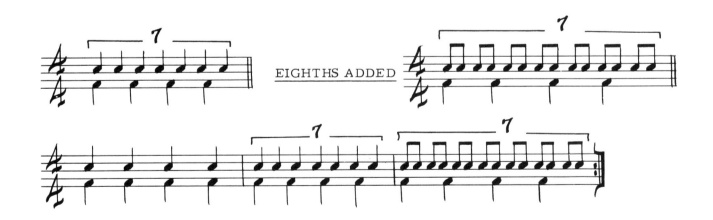

TRIPLETS

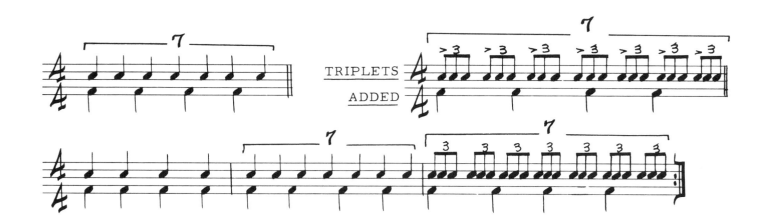

TRIPLETS
ADDED

EXERCISES

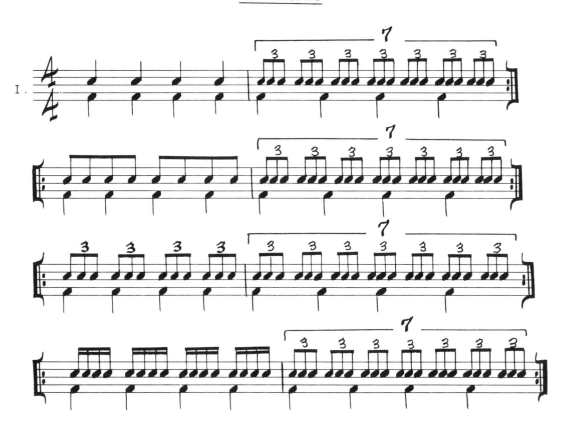

I.

EXERCISES (Cont.)

II.

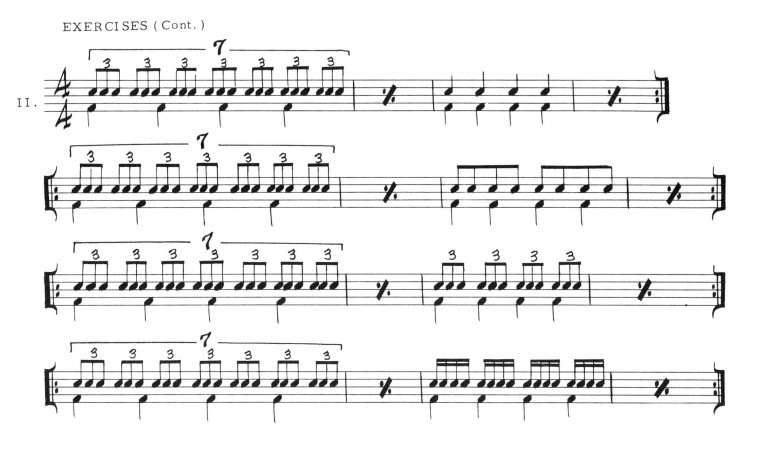

SIXTEENTHS

SIXTEENTHS
ADDED

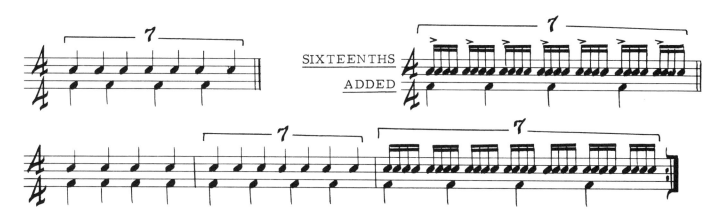

EXERCISES

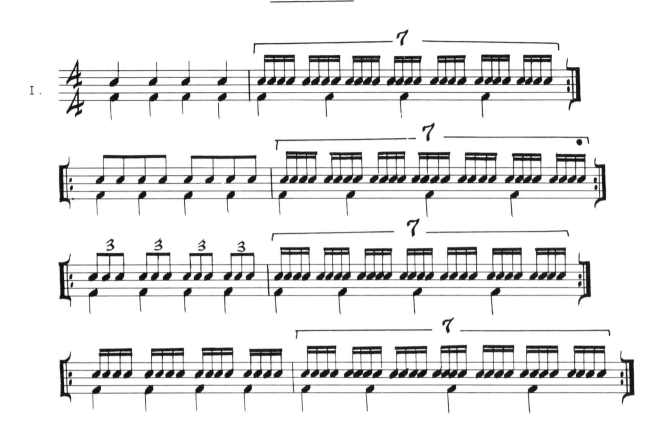

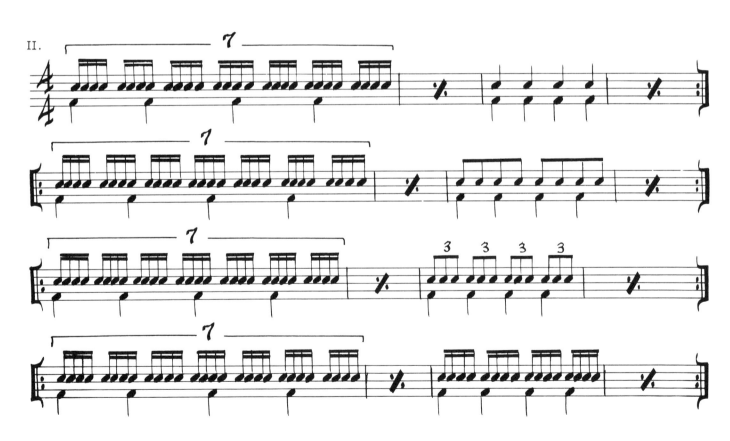

COMBINATIONS

MIXED COMBINATIONS

SOLO

SECTION 6

ELEVEN AGAINST FOUR

Two counting possibilities

AS WRITTEN:

EXERCISES

Keep an even tempo!

EIGHTHS

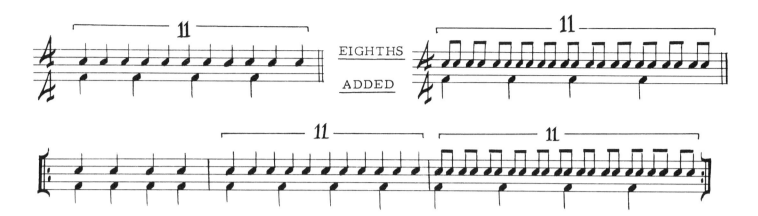

EXERCISES

EXERCISES (Cont.)

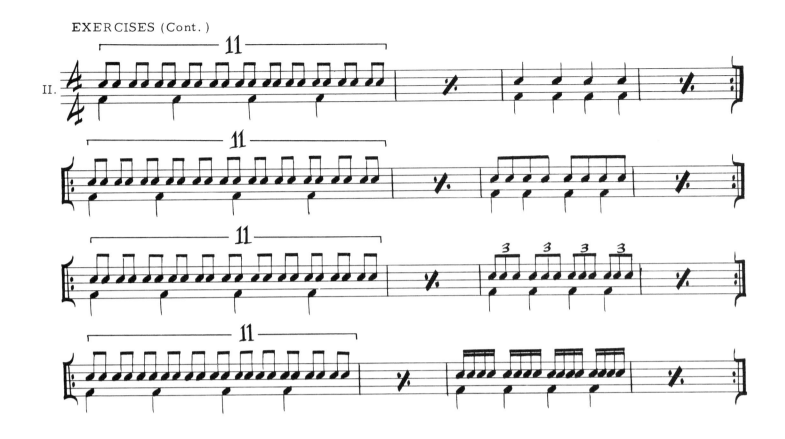

TRIPLETS

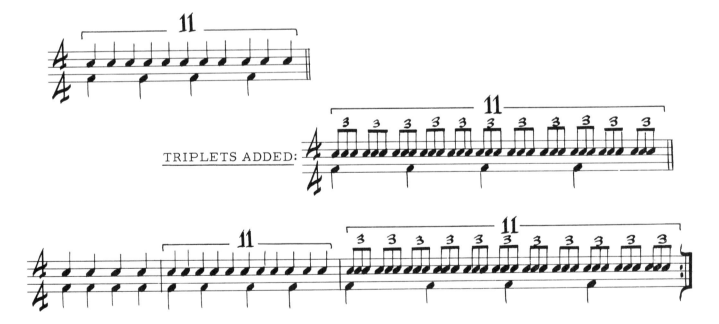

EXERCISES

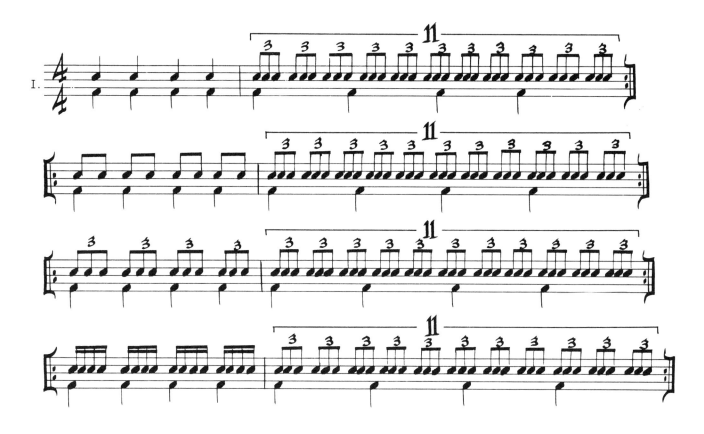

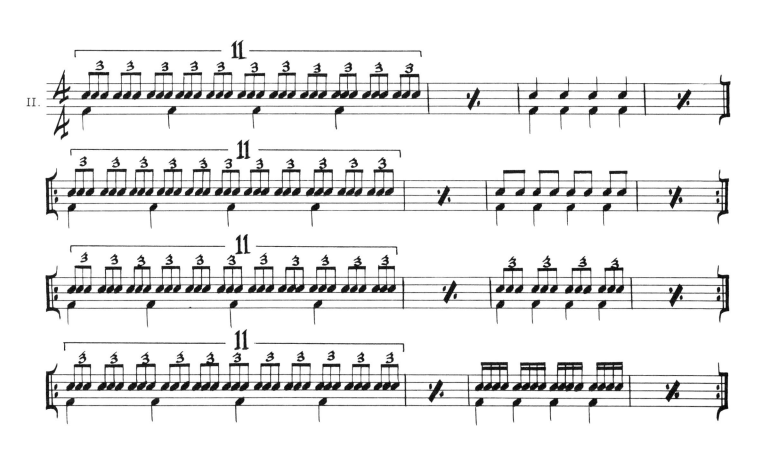

SIXTEENTHS

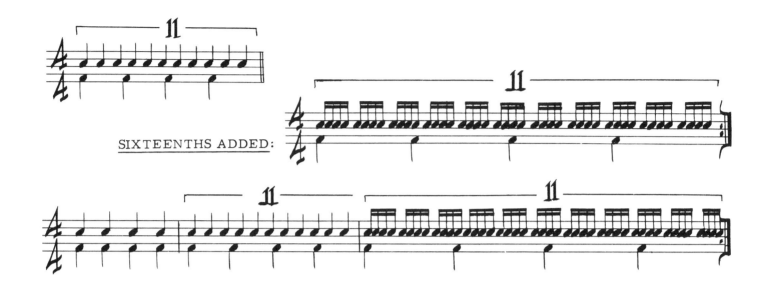

SIXTEENTHS ADDED:

EXERCISES

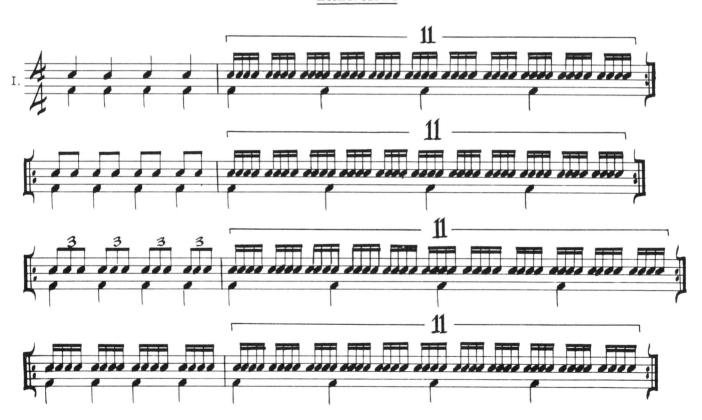

EXERCISES (Cont.)

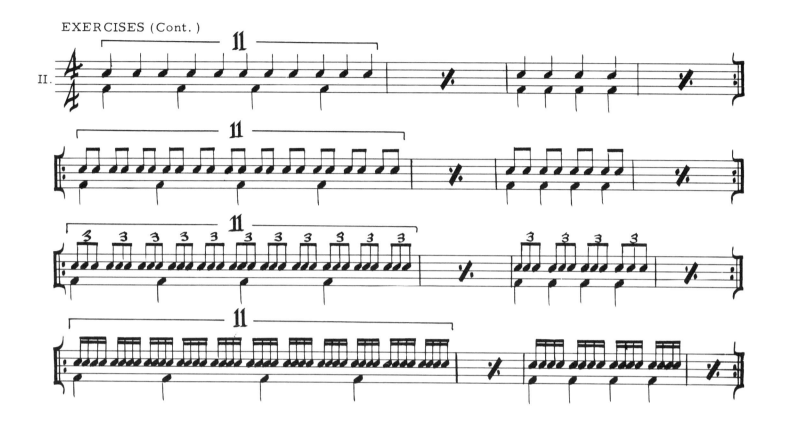

SHORT COMBINATIONS

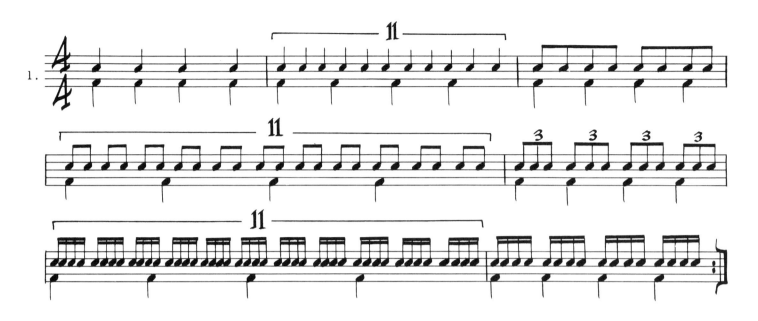

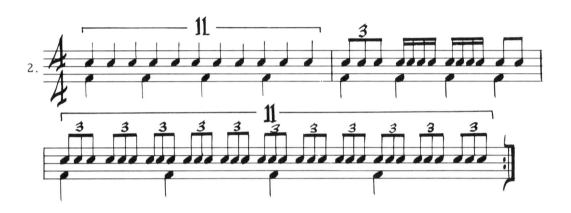

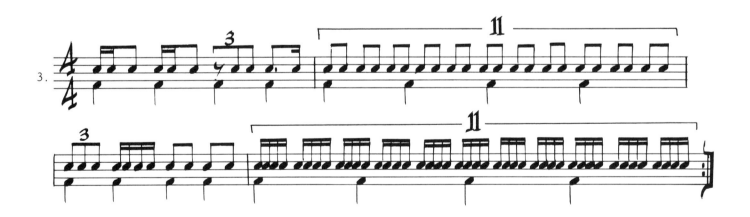

MIXED COMBINATIONS

MIXED COMBINATIONS (Cont.)

SOLOS

SOLOS (Cont.)

SECTION 7

THIRTEEN AGAINST FOUR

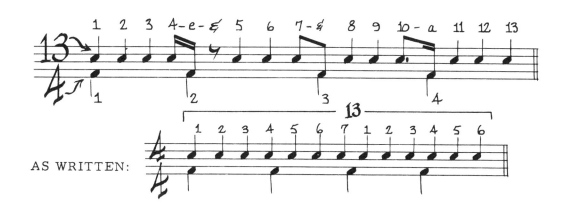

AS WRITTEN:

EXERCISES COMBINING 7, 11, and 13.

In all the following Exercises and Solos, all the counter rhythms are written against the "Basic Pulse" of four:

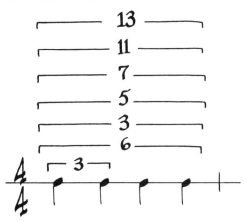

EXERCISES COMBINING 7, 11, and 13. (Cont.)

EXERCISES WITH RESTS

EXERCISES WITH RESTS (Cont.)

MIXED EXERCISES

SECTION 9

SOLO EXERCISES - 7, 11, and 13.

SOLO EXERCISES (Cont.)

SECTION 10

SOLO EXERCISES COMBINING 6, 3, 5, 7, 11, and 13.

SOLO EXERCISES (Cont.)

SOLO EXERCISES (Cont.)

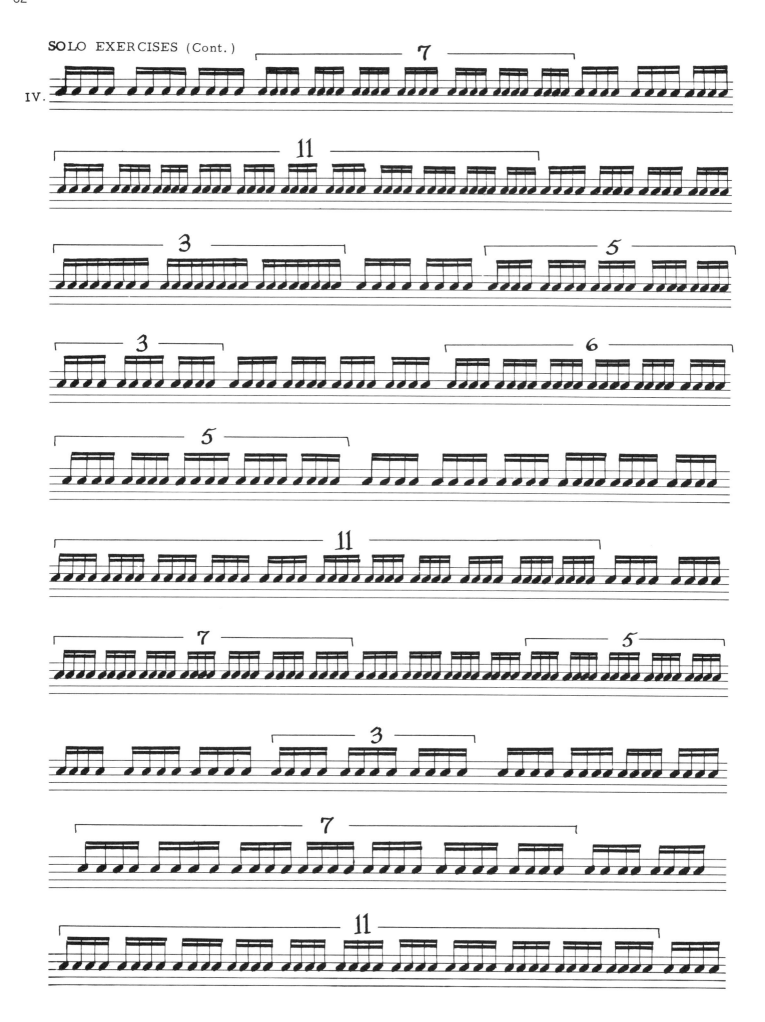

SOLO EXERCISES (Cont.)

SECTION 11

POLYRHYTHMIC TIME SIGNATURES

Polyrhythmic notation, as can be seen in the preceding pages, is usually accomplished by the use of brackets over the counter rhythm. Traditional time signatures make the bracket method an absolute necessity. It is possible, however, to add the information about the counter rhythm to the time signature. Admittedly, this would force a return to the restrictions of the bar line. If, however, the bar line were used only at points where a meter change occurred, it would, in effect, only stress those points where Basic Pulse and Counter Rhythm meet. The examples which follow are suggested as a logical method of indicating the metrical values of both voices of a polyrhythm in one time signature.

6 beats in Counter Rhythm.

4 beats in Basic Pulse.

Metrical unit of the basic pulse is the quarter note. When counter rhythm has <u>more</u> beats than the basic pulse, both are written in the same metrical unit. In this case the counter rhythm will be written as six quarter notes or the equivalent.

is identical with:

3 beats in Counter Rhythm.

4 beats in Basic Pulse.

Metrical unit of the basic pulse is the quarter note.

Should the counter rhythm be written in quarter notes, the measure would contain too few beats. When the counter rhythm contains fewer beats than the basic pulse, it must be written using the next longest metrical unit. In this case the counter rhythm would be written in half notes or the equivalent.

is identical with:

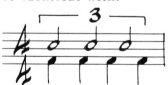

3 beats in Counter Rhythm.

 5 beats in Basic Pulse.

is identical to:

Basic pulse uses a metrical unit of eighth notes.

Counter rhythm will be written in quarter notes since it contains fewer beats than the basic pulse. (see above.)

 = Six quarters, or the equivalent, in a four/four measure.

 etc.

 = Three half notes, or the equivalent, in a four/four measure.

 = Three quarters, or the equivalent, in a four/eight measure.

 etc.

 = Four quarters, or the equivalent, in a six/eight measure

 = Three quarters, or the equivalent, in a two/four bar.

 etc.

 = Five eighth notes, or the equivalent, in a four/eight measure.

 etc.

66

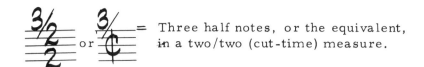 or  etc.

= Three half notes, or the equivalent, in a two/two (cut-time) measure.

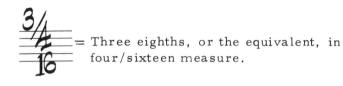 = Three eighths, or the equivalent, in four/sixteen measure.

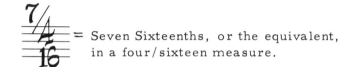 = Seven Sixteenths, or the equivalent, in a four/sixteen measure.

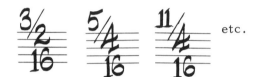 etc.

EXERCISES WITH POLYRHYTHMIC TIME SIGNATURES.